Thoughts that Make You Think

Keys to Everyday Living

Dr. Clarice Fluitt

Thoughts That Make You Think © 2015 Clarice Fluitt

All rights reserved. This publication is protected by the copyright laws of the United States of America. This publication may not be reproduced in any form, stored in a retrieval system, or transmitted in any form by any means; electronic, mechanical, photocopy, recording, scanning, or otherwise; without prior written permission of the author except as provided by United States of America copyright law. All rights reserved.

Publisher: Clarice Fluitt Enterprises, LLC
P O Box 15111
Monroe, LA 71207
www.claricefluitt.com

ISBN: 978-1-7331216-1-3

All rights reserved. For Worldwide Distribution

©Clarice Fluitt Enterprises• Distributed by Clarice Fluitt Enterprises, LLC •ClariceFluitt.com

Dedication

To my Heavenly Father who, only because of His saving grace, has brought me through the refiner's fire to become as gold and experience life and life more abundantly.

Acknowledgments

To my staff, Dr. Tandie Mazule, my Executive Assistant, and Dr. Evon Peet, my Administrative Assistant, whose diligence, perseverance, and insight have accomplished that which otherwise would have been impossible, I extend my deepest expression of thanks. It is true that without a vision people perish. Because of their participation in, passion for, and excitement about God's vision and purpose for this enterprise, that which was only a dream has now become a reality.

My Interior Designer, Carol Martinez, has become one of our own and brings dimension, character, and personality to every written page. My book would be incomplete without her expertise.

Endorsements

Dr. Clarice Fluitt is a woman with a relevant word deserving to be heard. Her ability to master the Master's language in multi-dimensional perspectives is a necessary sound to catapult this generation into epic encounters of reformational outcomes.

> Coach Anna McCoy,
> Author and Global Solutionist

Dr. Clarice Fluitt speaks truths that contain timeless wisdom. The blend of prophetic and revelatory insight imparts keys that anchor the heart, awakens the mind and shifts paradigms.

> Dr. Linda Wallace, Founder
> A Company of Women

Table of Contents

Part 1: *Make Your Deal Going In* 13

Part 2: *Dream, Action, Results* 23

Part 3: *Believe, Achieve, and Receive* 29

Part 4: *Developing Your Destiny* 41

Part 5: *We Are People in Transition* 47

Part 6: *The Greater the Change, the Greater the Reward* 57

Part 7: *Life Draws Life* 65

Part 8: *Honor Begins with You* 79

Part 9: *The Solution to Your Pollution* 87

Foreword

It has been said: "As a man thinks in his heart, so is he." In other words, we are who we are because of how we think. Our thoughts determine how we behave and how successful we become. Because this is true, the book you hold in your hands is an important resource for all who want to improve the way they think and what they think about.

Thoughts that Make You Think is the type of book you don't want to read quickly. You want to take a thought a day – or a week – and mull over it until your mind and heart can absorb each concept in such a way that you are changed from the inside out. The modern-day proverbs contained in these pages are written to arrest the mind; to stop it from simply glibly going over the words. Instead, there is an invitation to stop and ponder. One reads the thought and immediately considers: "What does this mean?" Or more importantly: "What does this mean to me? Should I do something about this?" The very act of thinking about it is the beginning of change. The entire book is an invitation, through pithy little phrases, to improve the quality of life you live, and through you, the quality of life of those you interact with.

Dr. Clarice Fluitt has shared keys that have brought her incredible success throughout her lifetime. She has proven that thinking rightly makes for an incredibly abundant and successful life. She herself is a thinker, but she doesn't stop at thinking. She puts thoughts into practice, and the results in her life have been amazing. She has been a highly successful businesswoman, with an enduring marriage and deep family relationships. Her life results come from the way she thinks and her thoughts are not theoretical, but very practical, with proven results. She has passed on keys that can also help you achieve similar results in your own life.

So if, in your busy, hectic life you feel like you have lost the ability to think deeply, then this book is for you. Put it in a visible place where you can pick it up often, perhaps many times a day, and think thoroughly through each concept. Read it slowly. Read it thoughtfully. Ask questions of yourself as you read. "Am I doing this? Could I do better?" You will benefit greatly from applying the wealth of wisdom found inside it. And you will enjoy the positive outcomes of thinking rightly in your daily life.

Stacey Campbell
Co-Founder of RevivalNow! Ministries and Praying the Bible International
Co-Senior Leader of New Life Church, B.C., Canada
Founder and Facilitator of the Canadian Prophetic Council
Honorary Member of the Apostolic Council of Prophetic Elders

Part One

Make Your Deal Going In

Thoughts that Make You Think

Champions live differently than ordinary people.
They don't run to run, they run to win.
Train to win the race set before you.

MY THOUGHTS

_____
_____
_____
_____
_____

Make Your Deal Going In

Pioneers live differently than settlers.

MY THOUGHTS

_____
_____
_____
_____
_____

*Don't settle. Run away from negative people.
Look out onto the sea of possibility
and take that step!*

MY THOUGHTS

_____
_____
_____
_____
_____

Make Your Deal Going In

You can do anything if it is important to you.

MY THOUGHTS

_____
_____
_____
_____
_____

*In life there is a thought, a word, and an action.
If you desire satisfaction, you should apply and
activate knowledge.*

MY THOUGHTS
_____
_____
_____
_____
_____

Make Your Deal Going In

Not to decide is a decision.

MY THOUGHTS
_____
_____
_____
_____
_____

Thoughts that Make You Think

*We are in a process, and the process
is as important as the product.*

MY THOUGHTS

_____
_____
_____
_____
_____

Make Your Deal Going In

Make your deal going in rather than trying to evaluate the loss factor after it has become impossible to recover.

MY THOUGHTS

Thoughts that Make You Think

Part Two

Dream, Action, Results

A person with an experience can be more valuable than a person who only has an opinion.

MY THOUGHTS

_____
_____
_____
_____
_____

Dream, Action, Results

Invest in your vision.
There has never been a farmer who got his field
plowed by only turning it over in his mind.

MY THOUGHTS

_____
_____
_____
_____
_____

If you desire the benefit of anything, you must embrace the procedure necessary to make it yours.

MY THOUGHTS

_____
_____
_____
_____
_____

If you want excellence, you have to plant excellence.

MY THOUGHTS

_____
_____
_____
_____
_____

Thoughts that Make You Think

Part Three

Believe, Achieve, and Receive

The curtain of opportunity goes up; the curtain of opportunity comes down.
Have you missed your opportunity? Another opportunity is calling your name ... can you hear?

MY THOUGHTS

_____
_____
_____
_____
_____

You will draw to yourself whatever you are releasing in the atmosphere with your countenance, conduct, and conversation.

MY THOUGHTS

_____
_____
_____
_____
_____

You may be down in the valley, but you don't need to drag others down there with you. Bring others up and guard your words; they come from the abundance of your heart.

MY THOUGHTS

_____
_____
_____
_____
_____

To the degree that you experience limitation, frustration, and humiliation you can be a candidate to experience exaltation without pride.

MY THOUGHTS

_____
_____
_____
_____
_____

Trying to please does not always produce pleasure.

MY THOUGHTS
_____
_____
_____
_____
_____

Every revelation brings a new revolution and a new set of friends.

MY THOUGHTS

_____
_____
_____
_____
_____

Thoughts that Make You Think

God will let you believe what you need to believe to get you where He's taking you.

MY THOUGHTS

_____
_____
_____
_____
_____

*Information without a revelation produces
imitation and leads to stagnation.
Revelation brings change, not repositioning.*

MY THOUGHTS
_____
_____
_____
_____
_____

Knowledge of a thing is not always a possession of the thing.

MY THOUGHTS
_____
_____
_____
_____
_____

Dare to believe. We are people making choices.

MY THOUGHTS

_____
_____
_____
_____
_____

Thoughts that Make You Think

Part Four

Developing Your Destiny

Without passion there is no power to pursue anything.

MY THOUGHTS

_____
_____
_____
_____
_____

Choose to get better and not bitter.

My Thoughts
___
___
___
___
___

A great life advisor is a guide that will know who you are and what you need so you can embrace the challenges for change.

MY THOUGHTS

_____
_____
_____
_____
_____

Life is for the living. Don't spend your life regretting. Forgive and forget. Press on.

MY THOUGHTS

_____
_____
_____
_____
_____

We should celebrate the greatness in those around us. And as we surround ourselves with those who also celebrate us and our lives, we can attain to greater heights through the process of intentional connections.

MY THOUGHTS

_____
_____
_____
_____
_____

Part Five

We Are People in Transition

*If you do not like what is going on in your life, you have the key to change,
but do you have the courage?*

MY THOUGHTS

_____
_____
_____
_____
_____

You can change your destiny anytime you are ready to do something new.

MY THOUGHTS

_____
_____
_____
_____
_____

So many times we hear something that sounds good and then say, "I think I will do this" and yet do nothing but think about it.

MY THOUGHTS
_____
_____
_____
_____
_____

A decision is not a conversion. Until you make a decision, a conversion cannot happen.

My Thoughts
_____
_____
_____
_____
_____

Do not just make mental ascent to truth but make the choice to do something you have never done before. Take a risk.

MY THOUGHTS

_____
_____
_____
_____
_____

You have to be willing to get up and do something that may not be comfortable or convenient."

MY THOUGHTS

_____
_____
_____
_____
_____

There are familiar things that we have grown accustomed to but they no longer serve our vision. They become a hindrance to our progress because we have outgrown them.

MY THOUGHTS

_____
_____
_____
_____
_____

*The moment you make a decision,
your destiny is born.*

MY THOUGHTS

_____
_____
_____
_____
_____

Thoughts that Make You Think

Part Six

The Greater the Change, the Greater the Reward

You can go fast, or you can go slow, but you're going to go even if you are bald headed with skid marks behind you because you resist.

MY THOUGHTS

_____
_____
_____
_____
_____

The Greater the Change, the Greater the Reward

If you desire the benefit of success,
you should begin to say what you want
and not what you feel.

MY THOUGHTS
_____
_____
_____
_____
_____

Where You lead I will follow, and what You feed I will swallow.

MY THOUGHTS
_____
_____
_____
_____
_____

The Greater the Change, the Greater the Reward

Every act of gratitude brings a refinement to your soul.

MY THOUGHTS

_____
_____
_____
_____
_____

Thoughts that Make You Think

*Meek does not mean weak,
but strength under control.*

MY THOUGHTS

The Greater the Change, the Greater the Reward

There is more to me than what you see.

MY THOUGHTS

_____
_____
_____
_____
_____

Immature does not mean impure.
Weak is not necessarily wicked.

MY THOUGHTS

_____
_____
_____
_____
_____

Part Seven

Life Draws Life

*Priorities should not compete with each other;
they must first be established and activated.*

MY THOUGHTS

_____
_____
_____
_____
_____

*Don't connect yourself with unhealthy
nonproductive relationships.
Choose your companions wisely.*

My Thoughts

_____
_____
_____
_____
_____

We must learn to avail and position ourselves for new opportunities.

MY THOUGHTS

_____
_____
_____
_____
_____

Opportunity travels with two faithful companions, fear and doubt.

MY THOUGHTS
_____
_____
_____
_____
_____

Nobody is exempt from troubles.

MY THOUGHTS

Life Draws Life

*Anything in your life that is shaken,
let it fall and let it go.*

MY THOUGHTS

_____
_____
_____
_____
_____

Thoughts that Make You Think

*You have seen the bitter,
but you shall soon know the sweet.
You know the fragmented,
but now you shall soon know the complete.
There is a victorious champion inside of you that
will soon be released.*

MY THOUGHTS

_____
_____
_____
_____
_____

Life Draws Life

The facts say you are oppressed, suppressed, repressed, depressed, and possessed. There's a difference between facts and truth. The truth says you are healed, delivered, and rich. Who will agree with God?

MY THOUGHTS

_____
_____
_____
_____
_____

I proclaim and decree that for every second I am oppressed I claim a soul for the Kingdom of God! I release the antidote to all negative situations.

MY THOUGHTS

_____
_____
_____
_____
_____

Sometimes tribulation comes to reveal to us that it's time to change.

MY THOUGHTS

_____
_____
_____
_____
_____

We must stop invoking the familiar spirits from our old sin nature. This is the season to get our mind off ourselves and begin to cast our care upon the Lord.

MY THOUGHTS

*Learn to turn any challenge, any grief, any sorrow
into a positive opportunity.
Don't waste your sorrow.*

MY THOUGHTS
___
___
___
___
___

Thoughts that Make You Think

Part Eight

Honor Begins with You

What you honor – good or bad – you will draw to yourself.

MY THOUGHTS

_____
_____
_____
_____

Honor transcends culture and condition.

MY THOUGHTS

_____
_____
_____
_____
_____

Dishonor is empowered by a rebellious spirit. When we have the attitude toward those in authority that ask the question, "Who died and made you king?" the outcome of your chosen path of rebellion will result in a very, very difficult journey.

MY THOUGHTS

_____
_____
_____
_____
_____

Honor Begins with You

Honor is a decision.

MY THOUGHTS

_____
_____
_____
_____
_____

Learn to Pay it Forward
Wherever you find people who honor you,
reciprocate with kindness.
Learn to pay it forward.

MY THOUGHTS

_____
_____
_____
_____
_____

Age has an advantage. Being finely aged means we don't lose value, our value only intensifies!

MY THOUGHTS

_____
_____
_____
_____
_____

Wisdom is the ability to use knowledge skillfully as we HONOR one another.

MY THOUGHTS

_____
_____
_____
_____
_____

Part Nine

God's Solution to your Pollution

God didn't call you to do. He called you to be.

My Thoughts

_____
_____
_____
_____
_____

Everything you are going to get from God is going to come from your positive Biblical confession.

MY THOUGHTS
_____
_____
_____
_____
_____

God will take you low so you can go high without pride.

MY THOUGHTS

_____
_____
_____
_____
_____

You can lose your pride and dignity but get your peace and deliverance.

MY THOUGHTS
_____
_____
_____
_____
_____

Let your crisis work for you, not against you.
Talk about the victory that is already yours.

MY THOUGHTS

_____
_____
_____
_____
_____

God's Solution to Your Pollution

*The joy of the Lord will get you anyplace.
If the enemy can get your joy,
he can get your stuff.*

MY THOUGHTS

_____
_____
_____
_____
_____

*Fear is the lack of confidence.
Fear always accompanies unbelief
and unbelief leads to destroying your faith.*

MY THOUGHTS

_____
_____
_____
_____
_____

God's Solution to Your Pollution

*To fear God is to worship God
and you become that which you adore.*

MY THOUGHTS

_____
_____
_____
_____

God has not made us brassy bold but gold bold.

MY THOUGHTS

*God is not who you think He is.
He is who He says He is.*

MY THOUGHTS

_____
_____
_____
_____
_____

The devil is defeated.
You have the keys to the Kingdom.
Open every door
Don't you understand?
It's time to explore
It's time to leave all the things you have known
And begin to act like you're full grown
Who would agree with God?

MY THOUGHTS

_____
_____
_____
_____
_____

God's Solution to Your Pollution

The solution to your pollution
is to apply the Word of God.
Breathe deep the breath of God.

MY THOUGHTS

_____
_____
_____
_____
_____

About Dr. Clarice Fluitt

Dr. Clarice Fluitt is a powerful international speaker and industry leader. She is a highly sought after personal advisor, author, and life strategist whose message brings inspiration and innovation to every audience she encounters. Dr. Fluitt's insight and delivery have solidified her position as a renowned motivational speaker and transformational voice impacting countless lives daily.

As a global trainer for more than four decades, Dr. Fluitt's success is based on her ability to help organizations thrive for real results. Her experiences as corporate and executive coach, entrepreneur and strategic consultant allow Dr. Fluitt to share her proven strategies for building customer value, creating revolutionary products, inspiring innovation, and generating sustainable growth. She takes the time to understand your organization and your audience, and delivers an informative and highly engaging presentation that will help you and your teams achieve results.

Dr. Fluitt has shared the stage with some of the world's most influential pioneers in the industry to include Steve Forbes, Suze Orman, Larry King, Michael J. Fox, Rudy Giuliani, Les Brown, Daymond John, Rick Belluzzo, Shaquille O'Neal, Joe Montana and many other legendary speakers. Dr. Fluitt's direct approach to transformation is crafted and customized to ensure that every audience is equipped with the tools they need to succeed in today's economy.

More Resources by Dr. Clarice Fluitt

Books
Ridiculous Miracles
The Law of Honor
Inspirational Insights
Living the Unhindered Life
Developing Your Limitless Potential

For information on Real Results Solutions Coaching and Mentoring packages:
Visit: www.realresults.solutions

Contact Information
Clarice Fluitt Enterprises, LLC
P O Box 15111
Monroe, LA 71207

Phone: 318.410.9788

E-mail: drclarice@claricefluitt.com

Websites:
www.realresults.solutions

www.claricefluitt.com